R Controlled Vowels

PHONICS ACTIVITY WORKBOOK

Danielle Johnson

TABLE OF CONTENTS

© Designed by Danielle

AR ER IR OR & UR

Complete each word by filling in the blanks.

c _ _ d	sh _ _ t	sh _ _ k
c _ _ n	sc _ _ f	c _ _ cle
h _ _ n	t _ _ tle	j _ _
spid _ _	flow _ _	g _ _ m

AR ER IR OR & UR

Complete each word by filling in the blanks.

socc___	f___k	sk___t
g___l	t___key	b___k
sh___ts	h___se	st___m
c___t	y___n	p___ty

AR ER IR OR & UR

Complete each word by filling in the blanks.

b__ger 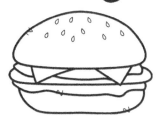	ott__ 	__m 
d__t 	sh___t 	hamm__ 
squ__t 	t__nip 	__t 
s__f 	sc__e Red Team: 7 Blue Team : 10	d__t 

AR ER IR OR & UR

Circle the word that matches the picture.

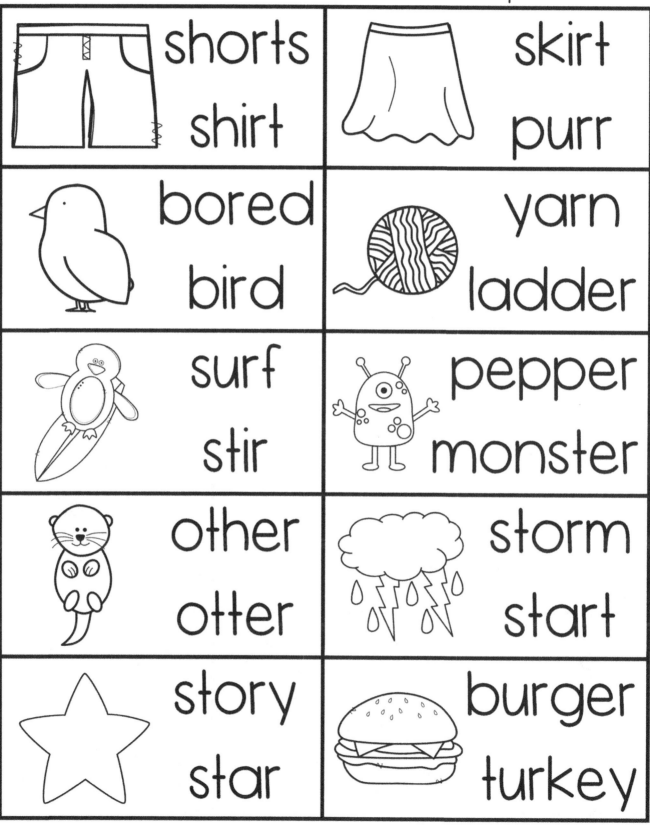

shorts	skirt
shirt	purr
bored	yarn
bird	ladder
surf	pepper
stir	monster
other	storm
otter	start
story	burger
star	turkey

Name:_____

AR ER IR OR & UR

Circle the word that matches the picture.

	store storm		jur jar
	turtle turnip		first surf
	marker farm		car corn
	hurt harp		litter letter
	dirt twirl		burn barn

AR ER IR OR & UR

Circle the picture that matches the word.

star	turtle
shorts	germ
shirt	turn
ladder	barn
fork	first
turnip	bird
bark	storm
finger	cart

AR ER IR OR & UR

Circle the picture that matches the word.

fur		burger	
spider		shark	
horn		termite	
skirt	THANK YOU	torch	
dirt		fern	
harp		car	
acorn		horse	
turkey		squirt	

9

© Designed by Danielle

AR ER IR OR & UR

Circle the picture that matches the word.

flower			
purse			
yarn			
girl			
store			
third			
scarf			
letter			

jar			
thorn			
monster			
burn			
twirl 30			
dart			
stork			
surf			

AR ER IR OR & UR

Color the AR words RED. Color the OR words BLUE.

red =AR Words   blue =OR Words

cart

Red Team: 7
Blue Team : 10

score

target

thorn

star

story

popcorn

harp

scarf

11

© Designed by Danielle

AR ER IR OR & UR

Color the AR words RED. Color the OR words BLUE.

red =AR Words   blue =OR Words

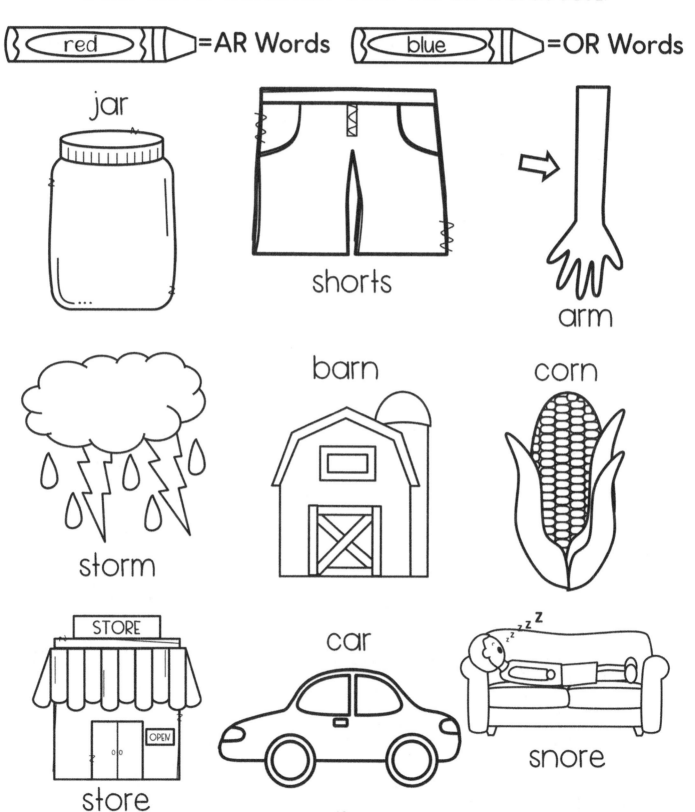

jar

shorts

arm

storm

barn

corn

STORE
OPEN

store

car

snore

© Designed by Danielle

Name:_____

AR ER IR OR & UR

Color the ER words RED, the IR words BLUE, and the UR words GREEN.

red =ER Words   blue =IR Words

green =UR Words

squirt

purr

otter

skirt

pepper

hammer

turtle

dirt

hurt

AR ER IR OR & UR

Color the ER words RED, the IR words BLUE, and the UR words GREEN.

red =ER Words   blue =IR Words

green =UR Words

shirt

monster

fur

first

termite

ladder

surf

turnip

bird

14

Name:_____

AR ER IR OR & UR

ar words

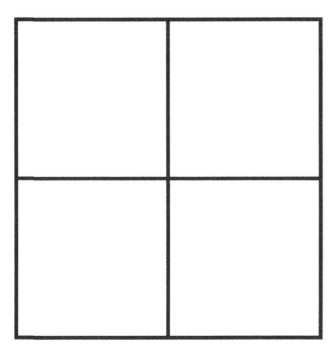

er words

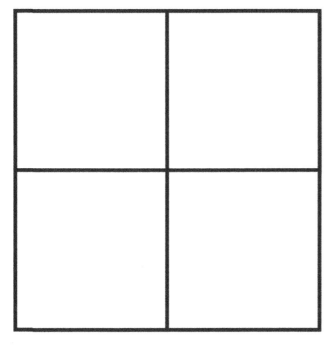

Cut out the pictures and paste them in the correct column.

g__m

c__d

THANK YOU

ladd___

sh__k

hamm__

st__

b__n

flow__

AR ER IR OR & UR

ir words

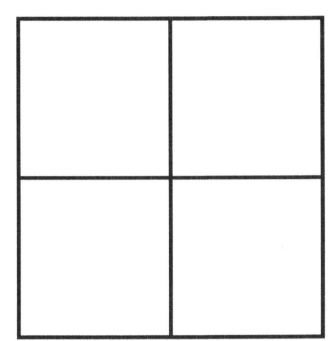

or words

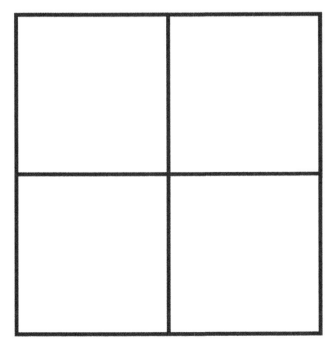

Cut out the pictures and paste them in the correct column.

h___se	sc___e
	Red Team: 7 Blue Team : 10
sh___t	st___m
f___st	d___t
sk___t	sh___t

© Designed by Danielle

Name:_____

AR ER IR OR & UR

ar words

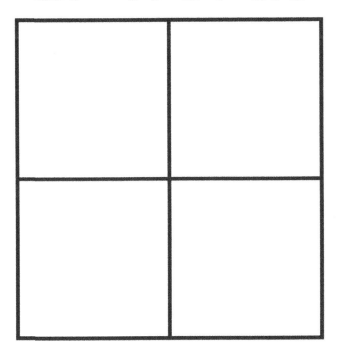

ur words

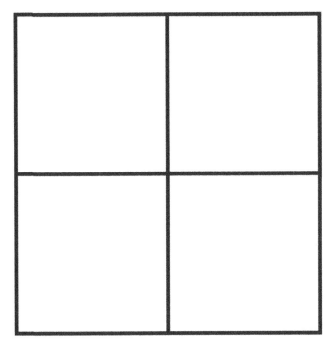

Cut out the pictures and paste them in the correct column.

t__tle

t__nip

j__

b__k

t__key

h__p

c__

s__f

© Designed by Danielle

AR ER IR OR & UR

er words

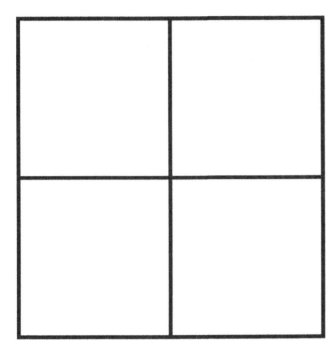

ir words

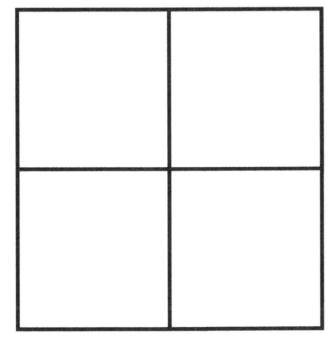

Cut out the pictures and paste them in the correct column.

th__d	spid__
monst__	g__l
blend__	b__d
th__ty **30**	pepp__

21

AR ER IR OR & UR

Cut out the words and sort them below. Read the words.

ar words

ir words

or words

ur words

stir
port
card
hurt
horn
skirt
first
fur
art
curl
more
start

Name:_____

AR ER IR OR & UR

Cut out the words and sort them below. Read the words.

ar words

er words

ir words

or words

chirp
charm
birth
term
born
herd
store
dark
skirt
her
cord
park

Name:_____

AR ER IR OR & UR

Cut out the words and sort them below. Read the words.

er words

ir words

or words

ur words

27

burn
sir
stern
dorm
after
stir
storm
hurt
firm
churn
germ
sore

© Designed by Danielle

AR ER IR OR & UR

Read each word and draw it.

art	snore	bird
hurt	first	spider
fork	dirt	barn

AR ER IR OR & UR

Read each word and draw it.

cart	turn	fort
torn	fern	nurse
germ	bark	burn

Name:_____

AR ER IR OR & UR

Cut out the letters and paste them into the correct box.

th☐ty   al☐m

sn☐e   p☐se

th☐n   m☐ble

| ar |
| ar |
| or |
| or |
| ir |
| ur |

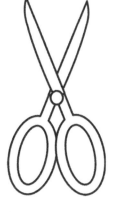

31

Name:_____

AR ER IR OR & UR

Cut out the letters and paste them into the correct box.

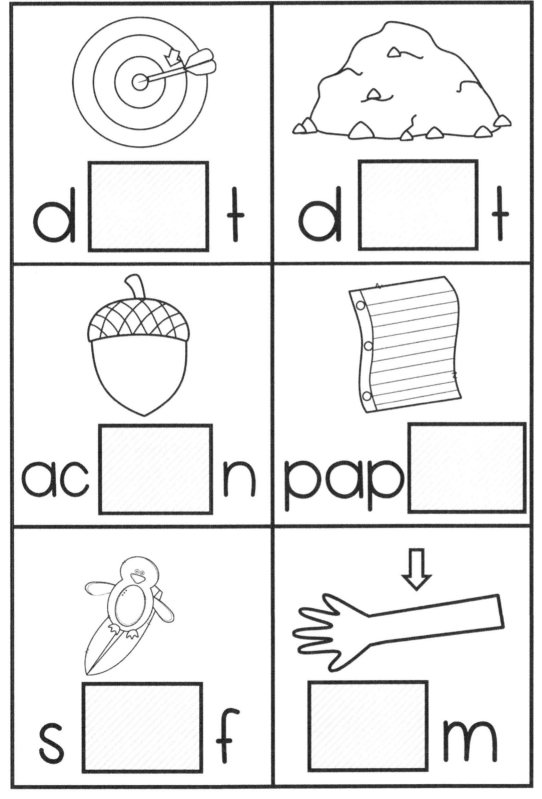

d ☐ t   d ☐ t

ac ☐ n   pap ☐

s ☐ f   ☐ m

ar
ar
or
er
ir
ur

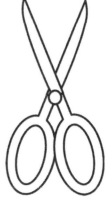

Name:_____

AR ER IR OR & UR

Cut out the letters and paste them into the correct box.

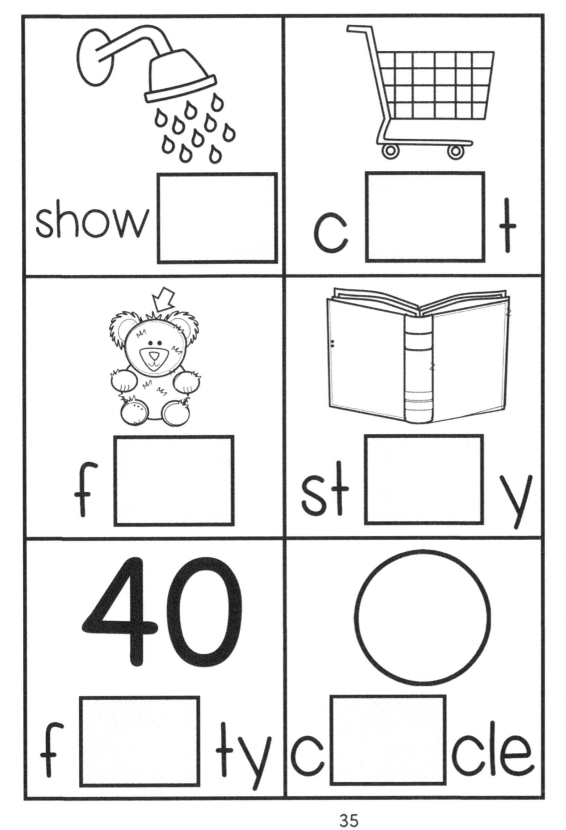

show[ ]

c[ ]t

f[ ]

st[ ]y

40

f[ ]ty

c[ ]cle

ar

er

ir

or

or

ur

AR ER IR OR & UR

Read the word. Trace the word. Write the word twice. Draw the word.

read/trace	write	draw
farm farm		
fort fort		
dirty dirty		
curl curl		
hammer hammer		

Name:_____

AR ER IR OR & UR

Read the word. Trace the word. Write the word twice. Draw the word.

read/trace	write	draw
dark dark		
cord cord		
bird bird		
hurt hurt		
tiger tiger		

38

© Designed by Danielle

AR ER IR OR & UR

Read the word. Trace the word. Write the word twice. Draw the word.

read/trace	write	draw
park park		
sport sport		
circle circle		
surf surf		
finger finger		

AR ER IR OR & UR

Read the sentence and illustrate it in the box.

There are birds in the park.	There is a spider in the jar.

The horse is wearing a scarf.	The paper is torn.

AR ER IR OR & UR

Read the sentence and illustrate it in the box.

The skirt has stars all over it.	A dog is barking at the stork.

The spiders are having a party.	There is a fork in her purse.

AR ER IR OR & UR

Use the word bank to fill in the blanks.

Word Bank:

turkey	horn	shark	torch	fork

circle	shorts	harp	paper

AR ER IR OR & UR

Use the word bank to fill in the blanks.

Word Bank:

first	bark	park	storm	water
bird	horse	corn	nurse	

_____

_____

_____

_____

_____

_____

_____

_____

_____

AR ER IR OR & UR

Draw lines to match the pictures to the words.

turnip

park

germ

scarf

burger

dirt

bird

corn

AR ER IR OR & UR

Draw lines to match the pictures to the words.

shorts

spider

surf

skirt

shark

thirty

storm

star

AR ER IR OR & UR

Draw lines to match the pictures to the words.

flower

harp

ladder

shirt

fork

turn

monster

yarn

46

AR ER IR OR & UR

Draw lines to match the pictures to the words.

car

horn

hammer

termite

turkey

stork

turtle

jar

AR ER IR OR & UR

Name:_____

Spell each word in the boxes.

card	forty	sports	nurse
third	letter	purse	dart

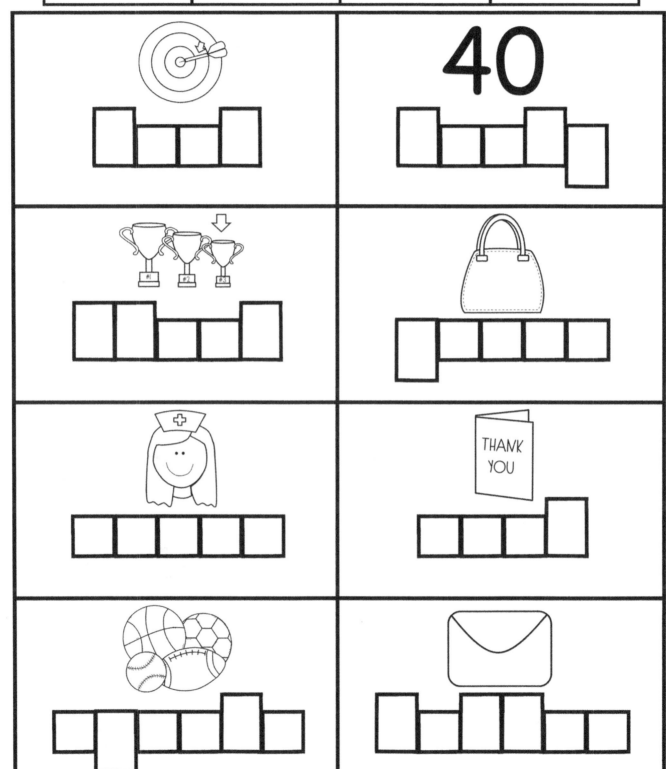

AR ER IR OR & UR

Name:_____

Spell each word in the boxes.

girl	barn	thorn	fur
store	burger	shower	cart

AR ER IR OR & UR

Name:_____

Spell each word in the boxes.

bird	horse	bark	shirt
arm	surf	turtle	paper

Name:_____

Cut out the words and paste them under the correct picture.

| turtle |
| party |
| storm |
| horn |
| jar |
| girl |
| shorts |
| water |

Name:_____

Cut out the words and paste them under the correct picture.

| flower |
| skirt |
| germ |
| soccer |
| scarf |
| finger |
| car |
| ladder |

53

© Designed by Danielle

Name:_____

AR ER IR OR & UR

Cut out the pictures and paste them next to the matching sentence.

The dog is barking at the horse.	
A red bird is on the car.	
The horse got first place in the race.	
My shorts have stars on them.	
The pig is having fun at the party.	

55

Name:_____

AR ER IR OR & UR

Cut out the pictures and paste them next to the matching sentence.

The bird has a purse.	
There are circles on the scarf.	
My horse can play the guitar.	
There is a spider in the jar.	
A stork has a fork in her bag.	

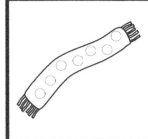

AR ER IR OR & UR
Read & Find

Name:_____

Read the word. Find the picture of the word. Circle the picture. Check off the word in the box.

monster ☐	corn ☐	skirt ☐	star ☐
circle ☐	storm ☐	turn ☐	torch ☐
turtle ☐	spider ☐	barn ☐	shark ☐

59

© Designed by Danielle

AR ER IR OR & UR
Read & Find

Read the word. Find the picture of the word. Circle the picture. Check off the word in the box.

termite ☐	bird ☐	shirt ☐	store ☐
blender ☐	purse ☐	car ☐	harp ☐
burger ☐	orange ☐	flower ☐	turkey ☐

Read & Find

Read the word. Find the picture of the word. Circle the picture. Check off the word in the box.

Name:_____

twirl	☐	turnip	☐	yarn	☐	fork	☐
germ	☐	first	☐	dart	☐	ladder	☐
surf	☐	shorts	☐	jar	☐	paper	☐

© Designed by Danielle

AR ER IR OR & UR

Read each sentence and underline all the words that have **ar** or **or** in them. Then write the words under the correct column below.

We drove the car to the farm.

Do you need a fork or spoon?

It is too hard to start it.

Plug in the cord.

When were you born?

---

ar words   or words

_____ | _____

_____ | _____

_____ | _____

_____ | _____

AR ER IR OR & UR

Read each sentence and underline all the words that have **ar** or **ur** in them. Then write the words under the correct column below.

Can you turn the alarm on?

I hurt my arm today.

My dog's fur is curly.

Let's play at the park.

It is going to get dark soon.

ar words   ur words

AR ER IR OR & UR

Read each sentence and underline all the words that have **er** or **ir** in them. Then write the words under the correct column below.

I was the first one to see her.

The bird was perched on the tree.

I do not like spiders.

Let's walk over to the circus.

When is your birthday?

er words   ir words

_____   _____

_____   _____

_____   _____

_____   _____

AR ER IR OR & UR

Use the word bank to fill in the blanks.

Word Bank:

hard	water	more
stir	dark	turn

It is too _____ in here.

I will _____ the soup.

_____ left at the corner.

The test was _____.

She drank some _____.

You have _____ than me.

© Designed by Danielle

AR ER IR OR & UR

Use the word bank to fill in the blanks.

Word Bank:

start	purple	third
burger	story	chores

He ate a _____ .

My favorite color is _____ .

Can we _____ the game?

We came in _____ place.

I need to do my _____ .

I read her a _____ .

Name:_____

AR ER IR OR & UR

Use the word bank to fill in the blanks.

Word Bank:

born	pepper	store
hurt	yard	dirty

My room is _____.

She _____ her leg at recess.

This _____ sells skirts.

The _____ has green grass.

He was _____ in July.

I'll pass the salt and _____.

© Designed by Danielle

AR ER IR OR & UR

Unscramble the words to make a sentence and write the sentence on the lines.

plays	He	at	park.
the	his	guitar	

She	scarf	party.	a
wore	the	to	

barn	is	horses.	The
of	full	brown	

AR ER IR OR & UR

Unscramble the words to make a sentence and write the sentence on the lines.

made	card	nurse.	I
a	for	my	

has	purple	girl	purse.
a	The		

ladder.	The	the	hammer
under	is		

© Designed by Danielle

AR ER IR OR & UR

Circle the word that makes sense in the sentence.

I live very _____ away.	far for
The jam was in the _____ .	jar tar
She got _____ when she fell.	hurt burn
We filled the _____ with food.	curt cart
My little sister was _____ today.	bird born
The kitten has a soft _____ .	purr stir
I really like _____ shirt.	were her

AR ER IR OR & UR

Circle the word that makes sense in the sentence.

I lost _____ of my homework.	port part
She made a left _____.	turn torn
My dad loves to sit on the _____.	porch par
I saw the band _____ on the field.	mart march
Will you _____ my hair?	carl curl
You need to _____ the batter.	stir storm
What is your favorite _____?	sport tore

Name:_____

AR ER IR OR & UR

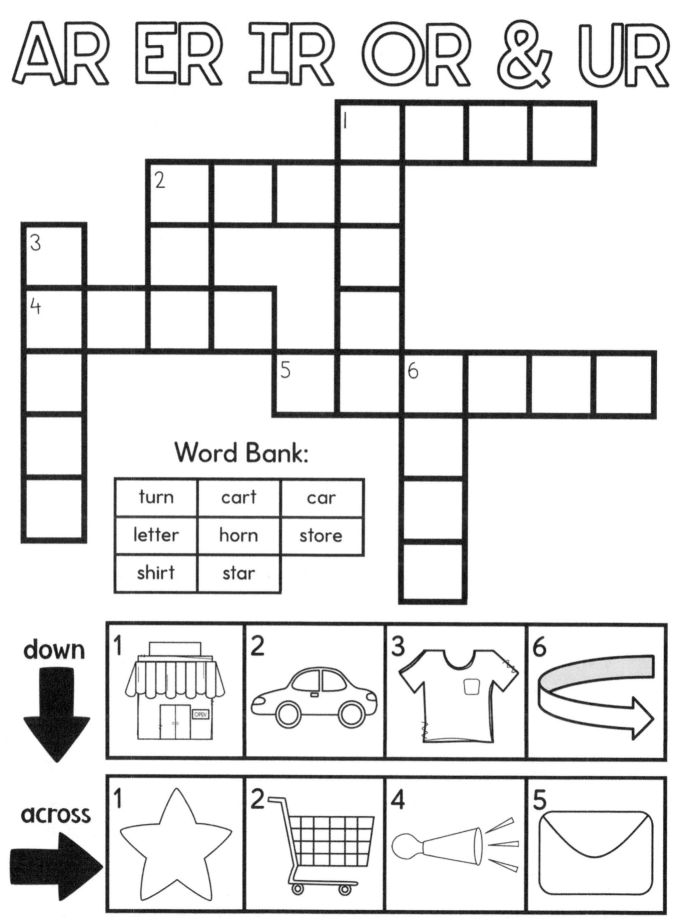

Word Bank:

turn	cart	car
letter	horn	store
shirt	star	

down

across

© Designed by Danielle

Name:_____

AR ER IR OR & UR

Word Bank:

first	surf	storm
art	fern	turnip
fur	sport	

down

across

© Designed by Danielle

AR ER IR OR & UR

Name:_____

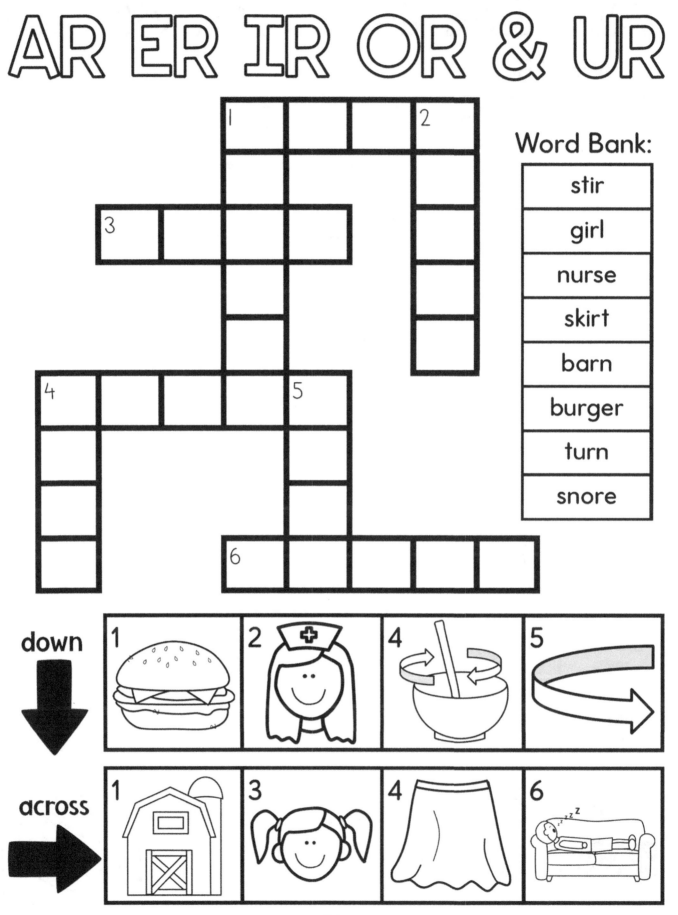

Word Bank:

| stir |
| girl |
| nurse |
| skirt |
| barn |
| burger |
| turn |
| snore |

down

across

AR ER IR OR & UR

party	card	purse	horse
stir	fork	butterfly	barn

	Across	Down
	2. friends get together and have fun	1. mix up
	3. give someone this on their birthday	2. keep a wallet and keys in here
	4. colorful insect	4. where horses sleep
	6. animal with four legs	5. eat food with this

Name:_____

AR ER IR OR & UR

Read the word and circle it in the word search.
Then write the word under the picture.

| car ☐ |
| skirt ☐ |
| barn ☐ |
| corn ☐ |
| dirt ☐ |
| burger ☐ |
| flower ☐ |
| surf ☐ |

f	r	u	s	e	c	y	n	z	m
b	t	a	s	r	o	a	q	w	t
u	s	d	q	x	r	b	t	v	r
r	f	b	a	r	n	r	e	w	i
g	c	p	v	t	j	k	l	c	k
e	d	e	b	h	x	z	u	q	s
r	y	t	r	i	d	w	i	o	o
g	g	u	f	l	o	w	e	r	p
h	f	i	n	c	a	r	m	j	k

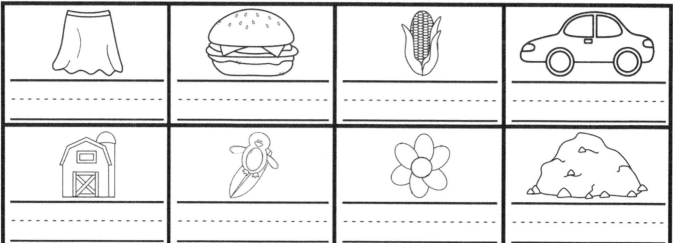

76

© Designed by Danielle

AR ER IR OR & UR

Read the word and circle it in the word search.
Then write the word under the picture.

| scarf ☐ |
| shirt ☐ |
| storm ☐ |
| turtle ☐ |
| yarn ☐ |
| hammer ☐ |
| circus ☐ |
| score ☐ |

y	a	r	n	m	r	o	t	s	g
q	m	z	h	y	e	u	z	i	x
x	r	p	t	e	r	l	h	v	d
c	g	o	j	l	o	k	a	f	c
s	h	i	r	t	c	o	m	r	b
r	e	w	f	r	s	u	m	a	c
r	d	e	w	u	i	p	e	c	n
t	a	b	s	t	v	q	r	s	g
n	c	i	r	c	u	s	y	s	m

Red Team: 7
Blue Team : 10

Name:_____

AR ER IR OR & UR

Read the word and circle it in the word search.

Then write the word under the picture.

| shorts ☐ |
| bird ☐ |
| first ☐ |
| star ☐ |
| letter ☐ |
| orange ☐ |
| purse ☐ |
| cart ☐ |

r	q	e	s	r	u	p	j	n	m
w	l	e	t	t	e	r	i	f	h
t	d	e	l	h	k	e	n	i	g
y	r	b	w	t	c	g	f	r	g
u	i	x	f	q	o	n	d	s	y
e	b	c	a	r	t	a	j	t	s
s	v	p	o	r	d	r	v	a	k
s	t	a	r	p	z	o	u	l	b
x	i	c	a	s	t	r	o	h	s

_____   _____   _____   _____

_____   _____   _____   _____

AR ER IR OR & UR

Name:_____

Cut out the words below and paste them to make a sentence.

I got a cart	
The bird	
I want more	
I tore my	
The jar was	
She hurt	

her left arm.	ate the worm.
purple skirt.	at the store.
candy corn.	hard to open.

© Designed by Danielle

AR ER IR OR & UR

Name:_____

Cut out the words below and paste them to make a sentence.

I forgot to go	
A thorn hurt	
I built my first	
That girl	
The farm is	
Don't burn the	

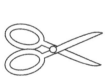

my finger.	to the store.
is a nurse.	paper.
blanket fort.	far away.

Name:_____

AR ER IR OR & UR
Color in AR or OR to make a word.

ch__e	ar / or	s__t	ar / or
sm__t	ar / or	m__t	ar / or
d__t	ar / or	sc__f	ar / or
m__ker	ar / or	__der	ar / or
st__m	ar / or	c__n	ar / or

© Designed by Danielle

AR ER IR OR & UR

Color in AR or OR to make a word.

st__t	ar / or	h__se	ar / or
t__n	ar / or	y__n	ar / or
h__m	ar / or	b__k	ar / or
sh__p	ar / or	h__n	ar / or
sp__t	ar / or	th__n	ar / or

AR ER IR OR & UR

Color in ER, IR, or UR to spell the word.

f__	er / ir / ur	th__ty	er / ir / ur
n__ve	er / ir / ur	t__tle	er / ir / ur
h__t	er / ir / ur	wat__	er / ir / ur
d__t	er / ir / ur	g__l	er / ir / ur
spid__	er / ir / ur	s__f	er / ir / ur

AR ER IR OR & UR

Color in ER, IR, or UR to spell the word.

p__se	er / ir / ur	t__mite	er / ir / ur
b__d	er / ir / ur	b__th	er / ir / ur
pepp__	er / ir / ur	b__n	er / ir / ur
tw__l	er / ir / ur	lett__	er / ir / ur
t__n	er / ir / ur	f__st	er / ir / ur

© Designed by Danielle

AR ER IR OR & UR

Roll and Read

part
fort
more
storm
first

form
ladder
fern
torn
bore

girl
harp
curve
park
turn

far
barn
thirst
burger
mark

hurt
party
dart
stork
dorm

shirt
cart
shark
hammer
turnip

© Designed by Danielle

Roll and Read

farm
start
part
far
scar

spider
fern
germ
ladder
finger

third
dirt
twirl
girl
birth

fort
story
port
storm
sport

hurt
turn
surf
purr
purse

curve
short
scarf
park
burner

Roll and Read

hard

mart

car

yard

large

perk

stern

were

termite

ladder

thirty

bird

circle

squirt

swirl

torch

forty

snore

score

bore

turtle

turkey

fur

hurt

burn

mark

dark

her

stir

dorm

Roll and Read

●	A girl helps the hurt turtle.
⚁	The horse is in the barn.
⚂	Put the corn in the cart.
⚃	Pack a shirt and shorts.
⚄	A nurse went up a ladder.
⚅	My letter is about the park.

© Designed by Danielle

Roll and Read

•	I ate a burger and corn.
::	The thorn hurt my finger.
:::	The shark saw the bird.
::::	The flower is in the dirt.
:::::	The storm is not far away.
::::::	There are thirty cars here.

© Designed by Danielle

Name:_____

Roll and Read

⚀	The paper is torn.
⚁	A dog barks at the spider.
⚂	This story is about otters.
⚃	Do not squirt the water.
⚄	The turtle is thirsty.
⚅	I like her purple purse.

AR ER IR OR & UR

Cut out the words. Then glue them in alphabetical order.

1. ☐   7. ☐

2. ☐   8. ☐

3. ☐   9. ☐

4. ☐   10. ☐

5. ☐   11. ☐

6. ☐   12. ☐

| purr |
| cart |
| far |
| stir |
| dorm |
| mark |
| yard |
| herd |
| turtle |
| bird |
| jar |
| order |

Name:_____

AR ER IR OR & UR

Cut out the words. Then glue them in alphabetical order.

1. [ ]   7. [ ]

2. [ ]   8. [ ]

3. [ ]   9. [ ]

4. [ ]   10. [ ]

5. [ ]   11. [ ]

6. [ ]   12. [ ]

| hard |
| for |
| turn |
| art |
| more |
| purse |
| curb |
| germ |
| start |
| burn |
| worn |
| dirt |

AR ER IR OR & UR

Cut out the words. Then glue them in alphabetical order.

1. [ ]   7. [ ]

2. [ ]   8. [ ]

3. [ ]   9. [ ]

4. [ ]   10. [ ]

5. [ ]   11. [ ]

6. [ ]   12. [ ]

large
curve
hurt
germy
nor
arm
dark
party
bark
mart
first
tart

AR ER IR OR & UR
Write a sentence using the given word.

part >---

----

other >--

----

first >--

----

torn >---

----

curb >---

© Designed by Danielle

AR ER IR OR & UR

Write a sentence using the given word.

hard ⟩------------------------------------

pepper ⟩------------------------------------

shirt ⟩------------------------------------

for ⟩------------------------------------

turn ⟩------------------------------------

AR ER IR OR & UR
Write a sentence using the given word.

farm

blender

bird

more

hurt

Name:_____

AR ER IR OR & UR
Write a sentence using the given word.

start

marker

girl

storm

fur

© Designed by Danielle

Farm

Cut out the pictures below and paste them next to the correct word in the story. Then read the story.

My farm is great! It has a nice

barn [ ] where the <u>horses</u> [ ]

stay. It also has a <u>corn</u> [ ] field

and many beautiful <u>flowers.</u> [ ] I

love laying in the field and looking up

at the <u>stars.</u> [ ] Sometimes I lay

there for hours! I always see a

<u>butterfly</u> [ ] or two fly by.

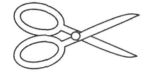

Dinner

Cut out the pictures below and paste them next to the correct word in the story. Then read the story.

Thanksgiving dinner with my family is

so much fun. The best part is the

turkey, [ ] but I also like the corn. [ ]

I try to be first [ ] in line to fill my plate

because I don't want to wait for my

turn. [ ] I fit as much food on my

fork [ ] as I can. I usually forget to

drink my water [ ] because the food

is so yummy!

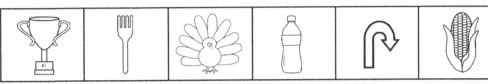

© Designed by Danielle

Made in the USA
Las Vegas, NV
03 April 2025